## Background

It is important that parents take resp[illegible] their children's teeth. This is a combination of oral health at home a[illegible]e dentist. It is helpful for children to get used to visiting the dentist from an ea[illegible] [illegible]omes part of their normal routine. This will help support growing teeth by monitoring their development.

It is completely normal for some children, especially those who are neurodivergent, and those who have additional needs, to feel anxious about visiting the dentist for the first time. It is a new and unfamiliar place, and some children may be sensitive to bright lights, sounds and touch. This book is here to offer gentle support and to help make the experience feel less overwhelming and more manageable.

The story guides children through what to expect when they arrive at the dentist, helping them to feel more comfortable with what they might see and do. There is a fun, step-by-step visual guide to show the best way to keep teeth and gums healthy; extra tips to support parents and carers; plus instructions on how to clean teeth and gums too!

With thanks to the Oral Health Promotion Team at the Sussex Community NHS Foundation Trust for their advice on the current national guidance on toothbrushing (2025).

Other Books in the Series

# Meet the Characters

## New Words

| | | |
|---|---|---|
| Decay | 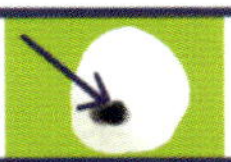 | Damage caused by not cleaning teeth properly or too much sugar. |
| Filling |  | A special material the dentist uses to fill a hole. |
| Fluoride |  | Is added to toothpaste to prevent tooth decay. |
| Mouth mirror |  | A small mirror used by the dentist to see all of your teeth, closely. |
| Varnish |  | A special protective coating containing fluoride, used by the dentist. |

# Hedgy Visits the Dentist

**Binkie & Friends' Adventures**

Written by Julie Alison McDonald & Anna Emilia
Illustrated by Julie Alison McDonald

"I'm curious," says Hedgy, "as I've somewhere new to go,
I'm off to see the dentist soon, is this a place you know?"

He asks his good friend Binkie, “Tell me, what’s it like there?”
“The dentist’s really kind and you’ll like the special chair!”

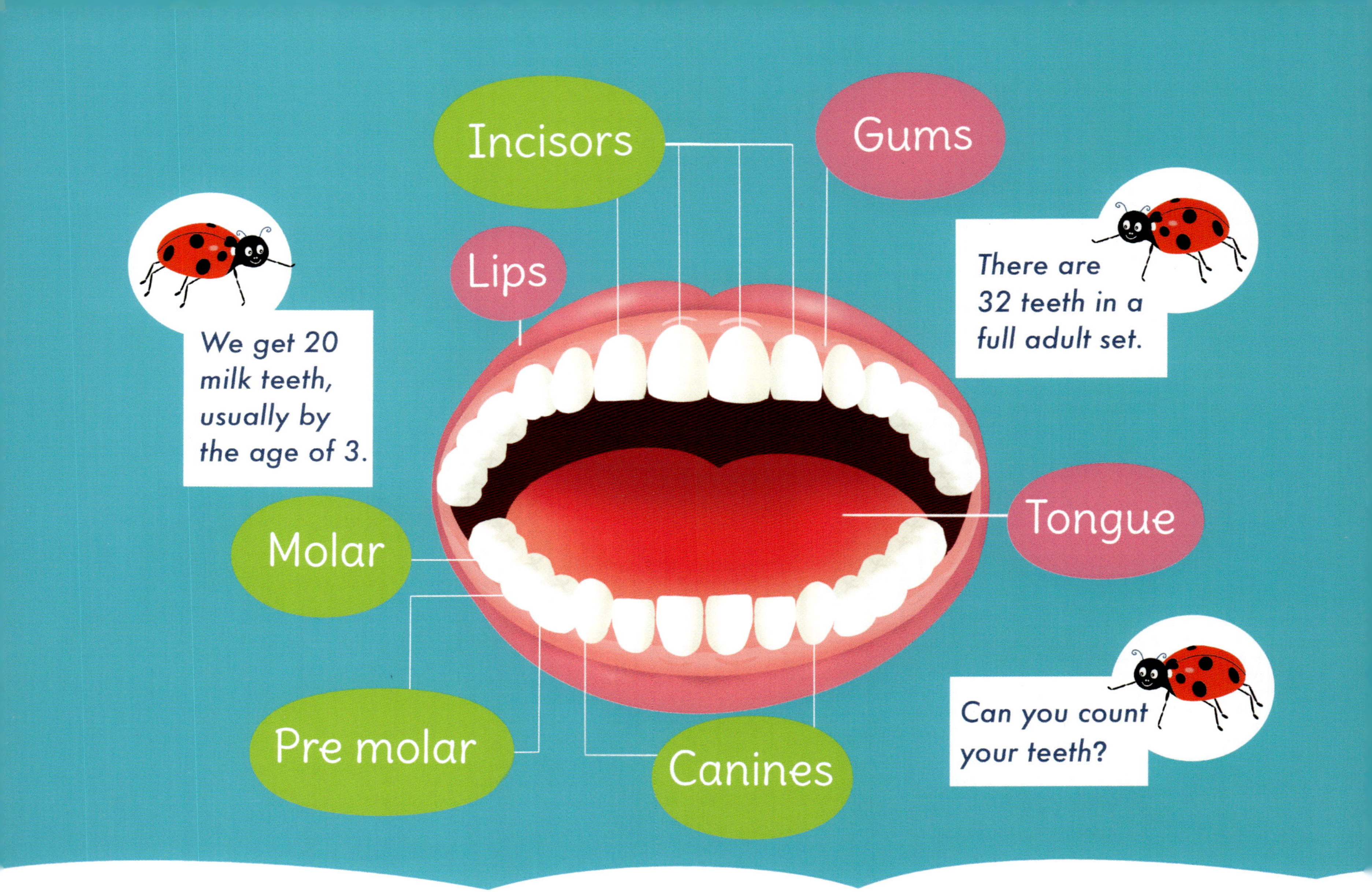


"It's where the dentist checks your teeth, to see if they're okay,
To count how many teeth you have, make sure there's no decay."

Today is Hedgy's check-up, it's this afternoon at four,
He quickly grabs his ear pads as he's leaping out the door.

The tortoise at the welcome desk greets clients with a smile,
They wait for their appointments, which can take a little while.

They read the posters on the wall and chat with others too,
The nurse calls Hedgy's name out next, it's time now to go through.

Sadie smiles so kindly and explains what to expect,
Hedgy now feels happy now he knows what's coming next.

Once Hedgy's lying in the chair it makes a funny sound,
His feet rise up, his head tilts back, it raises from the ground.

Now wearing special goggles Hedgy opens his mouth wide,
Then Seb turns on a beaming light as Sadie looks inside.

Sadie counts up Hedgy's teeth and then inspects his tongue,
Next she feels inside his cheeks and presses on his gums.

“If the mirror feels too cold, or if you’d like a break,
Please put up your hand and give it a gentle shake.”

"We're now nearly finished, there's just one more step to go,
You might find this tickles, if it's too much let me know."

Sadie paints on varnish with a soft and silky brush,
Hedgy likes the smell and taste, his teeth are looking lush.

Now Hedgy gets a sticker as he's been so very brave,
As Seb and Sadie say "goodbye" they give a little wave.

So, if you want to keep your teeth strong and healthy too,
Follow Hedgy's five step plan, he'll show you what to do!

# 1

Choose the right toothpaste,
Make sure you like the taste.
Squeeze some on a dry toothbrush,
It's good to leave no waste.

Some toothpastes don't foam.

Some toothpastes are flavourless.

## Ages 0 - 3

Use a smear of toothpaste, the size of a grain of rice.

## Ages 3+

Use a pea-sized amount of toothpaste.

Don't eat or drink for 30 minutes either side of brushing your teeth.

# 2

Brush at least twice a day,
Two minutes at a time,
Firstly in the morning,
Then, once before bedtime.

Brush in the morning

Brush before bedtime

## 3

Don't rinse your mouth,
All you need to do is spit,
The magic will keep working,
So your teeth stay very fit!

Don't eat for 30 minutes before or after brushing.

Fluoride is the magic ingredient that protects your teeth.

# 4

Between lunch and dinner,
Healthy snacks are most ideal,
When you have a sweet food,
Try to eat it with your meal.

## In between Meals

Healthy snacks

Water

Milk

## Sweet Foods with Meals

+

5

So try to see your dentist,
At least once every year,
To keep your teeth squeaky clean,
Sparkling white and clear.

Visit your dentist at least once a year.

# MAZE

Help Hedgy to remember the steps.

How much toothpaste should I use?

For how long and how often should I brush my teeth?

What should I do after brushing my teeth?

Which snacks can I have between meals?

How often should I see the dentist?

Spit

At least once a year.

A healthy snack, milk or water.

Two minutes each time, twice a day.

No more than a pea-sized amount.

To check your answers, follow the wavy lines with your finger.

# PICTURE PLAN

## A quick reminder of what to expect:

You may have to wait a short while.

The dentist checks your teeth.

Then it's time to go home.

## How do I let the dentist know if I need a break?

Put up your hand and give it a shake.

OR

Use a card.

# GENERAL TIPS FOR PARENTS

The key to a successful first dental visit is preparation, communication and working with a supportive dental team who understands your child's needs.

Find a dentist ↓

- First Visit - the British Society of Paediatric Dentists currently recommends parents bring their child to the dentist when their first tooth arrives, or, by age one, whichever is earlier.

- Role Play - pretend to be the dentist. Ask your child to open their mouth wide, peer inside and count their teeth. Describe the bright lights, make sounds they might hear at the dentist and describe an imaginary tool you are holding that may touch their teeth - ie. a mirror on a stick. Then swap roles.

- Positive Language - explain that a dentist is a kind person who helps look after teeth and makes them stronger. Try to be relaxed as children are often good at picking up on their parents' moods.

## TIPS - BEFORE YOUR VISIT

- Talk to your dentist and let them know about your child's additional needs. You could ask for an appointment time when the practice is less crowded to avoid over stimulating your child; you might even need to see a specialist dentist.
- Arrange a 'pre-visit' so your child can become familiar with the environment and meet some of the staff. Alternatively, look at some images of the dental practice on the website.

## TIPS - ON THE DAY

- If your child has a comfort/sensory toy or wears ear defenders, make sure these are brought along.
- On the morning of your child's first dental appointment, remind them of what to expect by using Hedgy's picture plan.
- Praise your child during and after the visit, letting them know how proud you are.

# Learn how Hedgy cleans his teeth

1

Brush your teeth like Hedgy,
And you'll keep them just like new,
Now listen really carefully,
I'll show you what to do.

2

Squeeze toothpaste on your brush,
A pea-sized splodge or so,
Open your mouth really wide,
Ready steady go....

3

Start by brushing at the top,
Then move from left to right,
Making small round circles,
Soon your teeth will shine so bright!

4

Gently brush your gums as well,
The backs of your teeth too,
Clean the tops of molars,
These teeth really help you chew.

5

When your top teeth are all done,
It's time to brush below,
So, open your mouth really wide,
Ready, steady, go...

6

Give your bottom teeth a brush,
Then move from left to right,
Making small round circles,
Soon your teeth will shine so bright!

7

Gently brush your gums as well,
The backs of your teeth too,
Clean the tops of molars,
These teeth really help you chew.

8

Spit the toothpaste in the sink,
Then give yourself a cheer,
Your teeth are now squeaky clean,
Sparkling white and clear!

Now it's your turn! Start at step 1 and work your way through to step 8.